RIDICULOUS CUSTOMER COMPLAINTS (And other statements)

VOLUME 1 (Believe me this needs more than one volume)

By David Loman

"The customer is always right" or so anyone or has ever worked in any service industry is repeatedly told. In this book I have set out prove that statement is completely untrue and in fact with customers like these then maybe the opposite could be said.

So sit back, grab your self a drink perhaps an alcoholic one if you feel that way inclined and enjoy some of the strangest, ridiculous and most outrageous complaints and statements from all walks of life.

TRAVEL

We all long for the beach or perhaps an activity break. Holiday or vacation time is important to us mere humans and we are going to make damn sure we get what we paid our hard earned money for.

So on that note here are some of our favourite cruise complaints:

The sea sounding of the sea, who would have thought it?

The first comes from a woman on a Mediterranean cruise. She complained about the sea being too loud, claiming it had prevented her from having a decent night's sleep during her holiday on board. She also suggested that the cabins be "better sound-proofed against the sounds of the sea."

You just cannot get psychic staff these days.

A gentleman on a two-week Caribbean honeymoon cruise with his wife complained about the lack of ceremony accorded the couple's newly wed status. He expected the staff on board to dress their cabin in white, strew rose petals for them each morning and deliver champagne and strawberries each day via a private butler. The grousing groom admitted that he didn't request the measures in question, but expected the staff to know the couple were just married and offer special treatment accordingly, at no extra cost.

Flying must be the only way to travel abroad?

A woman on a cruise departing from Southampton (UK) informed the travel agency that she had been forced to reschedule her cruise holiday after failing to bring her passport with her when she turned up to board the ship. She believed she only needed her passport when going on a fly-cruise, and blamed the cruise company for not texting her the day before to remind her to take the document.

Everyone will be happy to wait for you, I'm sure.

A couple on a Mediterranean cruise complained about their captain being "rude" and selfishly failing to comply with their plans, despite them leaving him a detailed note. The couple left the note for the Captain in the morning to let him know they would be returning to the ship two hours later than the planned departure time due to having "too much to do in-port," but the Captain chose not to wait, departing as scheduled. The couple were forced to catch up with the ship at its next port stop the following day — and wanted compensation for their accrued travel costs.

Well you never know!

A young woman on a Hawaiian cruise contacted the customer service department and demanded to know why she didn't see Gary Barlow on her cruise. She explained that she had "heard that Gary Barlow was once on the same cruise" and that she expected to see him on her cruise, as well.

Maybe she has a point

A woman on a Celebrity Cruises ship asked for a full refund in June last year, simply because she didn't see any celebrities on board. According to her comments, the company was guilty of false advertising due to the lack of actual celebrities on the ship.

Ah, Alaska that well known hot spot, it's in the Caribbean isn't it?

A man who voyaged on a summer cruise around Alaska complained about the weather: It wasn't as warm as he'd expected. According to the disgruntled passenger, "all cruises are meant to be hot." The man then demanded compensation for having to buy warmer clothing — as he "had only packed minimal clothing for the expected hot weather"— explaining that his expectations of being able to swim in the swimming pool each day and "get an impressive tan" had not been met.

Did they request a tartan blanket and a flask of tea as well?

An elderly couple who went on a cruise around France and Spain asked for a full refund because the team on-board did not provide them with a packed lunch each day, after arriving in port, to take with them when leaving the ship.

Where are the rude staff when you need them?

A couple from Yorkshire contacted their travel agency to complain about the kindness of the staff on-board their cruise in October, explaining that they had to spend "a lot more money than planned in tips due to the excellent service." The couple were seeking some compensation for the cost of the tips given out.

The clue is in the description.

In January this year a woman called to express her disappointment with her inside cabin not having a window to the sea. Furthermore, she said, she couldn't understand why nobody on-board was able to install a window for her so she could enjoy the view, and she expected better service next time.

An aquarium cruise, not a bad idea.

A couple were disappointed when they booked an ocean view cabin on the bottom deck. They had expected to see fish swimming outside their window and were disappointed to only see the ocean.

It's not only cruise ship passengers that have a weird and wonderful list of complaints and requests, there are plenty of alternative ones too. Here are some of our favourite travel agency stories.

I'll have the least windy seat please.

A travel agent had someone ask for an aisle seat so that their hair wouldn't get messed up by being near the window.

An easy mistake to make.

I got a call from a woman who wanted to go to Cape town. I started to explain the length of the flight and the passport information when she interrupted me with "I'm not trying to make you look stupid, but Cape town is in Massachusetts. "Without trying to make her look like the stupid one, I calmly explained, "Cape cod is in Massachusetts, Cape town is in Africa." Her response ... click.

Florida – The narrow state

A man called, furious about a Florida package we did. I asked what was wrong with the vacation in Orlando. He said he was expecting an ocean-view room. I tried to explain that is not possible, since Orlando is in the middle of the state. He replied, "Don't lie to me. I looked on the map and Florida is a very thin state."

Damn those maps and their scales.

I got a call from a man who asked, "Is it possible to see England from Canada?" I said, "No." He said "But they look so close on the map."

Taking statements literally.

Another man called and asked if he could rent a car in Dallas. When I pulled up the reservation, I noticed he had a 1-hour lay-over in Dallas. When I asked him why he wanted to rent a car, he said, "I heard Dallas was a big airport, and I need a car to drive between the gates to save time."

Supersonic travel!

A nice lady just called. She needed to know how it was possible that her flight from Detroit left at 8:20am and got into Chicago at 8:33am. I tried to explain that Michigan was an hour ahead of Illinois, but she could not understand the concept of time zones. Finally I told her the plane went very fast, and she bought that!

I have the same problem when I fly into Dickinson Airport.

A woman called and asked, "Do airlines put your physical description on your bag so they know who's luggage belongs to who?" I said, "No, why do you ask?" She replied, "Well, when I checked in with the airline, they put a tag on my luggage that said FAT, and I'm overweight, is there any connection?" After putting her on hold for a minute while I "looked into it" (I was actually laughing) I came back and explained the city code for Fresno is FAT, and that the airline was just putting a destination tag on her luggage.

Screens sir, screens.

I just got off the phone with a man who asked, "How do I know which plane to get on?" I asked him what exactly he meant, which he replied, "I was told my flight number is 823, but none of these darn planes have numbers on them.

Advancement in airline technology.

"A woman called and said, "I need to fly to Pepsi-cola on one of those computer planes." I asked if she meant to fly to Pensacola on a commuter plane. She said, "Yeah, whatever."

That'll do nicely.

A business man called and had a question about the documents he needed in order to fly to China. After a lengthy discussion about passports, I reminded him he needed a visa. "Oh no I don't, I've been to China many times and never had to have one of those." I double checked and sure enough, his stay required a visa. When I told him this he said, "Look, I've been to China four times and every time they have accepted my American Express."

On safari.

A woman called to make reservations, "I want to go from Chicago to Hippopotamus, New York" The agent was at a loss for words. Finally, the agent: "Are you sure that's the name of the town?" "Yes, what flights do you have?" replied the customer. After some searching, the agent came back with, "I'm sorry, ma'am, I've looked up every airport code in the country and can't find a Hippopotamus anywhere." The customer retorted, "Oh don't be silly. Everyone knows where it is. Check your map!" The agent scoured a map of the state of New York and finally offered, "You don't mean Buffalo, do you?" "That's it! I knew it was a big animal!"

As you have seen in the previous examples the public do have some very strange ideas about travel. But it is not just the agents who receive these. Here are a selection of the best and worst of complaints to tour operators.

What no digestives!

"I think it should be explained in the brochure that the local store does not sell proper biscuits like custard creams or ginger nuts."

There's no fiesta in a siesta.

"It's lazy of the local shopkeepers to close in the afternoons. I often needed to buy things during 'siesta' time - this should be banned."

Hold the chilli powder.

On my holiday to Goa in India, I was disgusted to find that

almost every restaurant served curry. I don't like spicy food at all."

Skinny dipping?

"We booked an excursion to a water park but no-one told us we had to bring our swimming costumes and towels."

To be fair that is enough to make anyone feel inadequate.

A tourist at a top African Game Lodge over looking a water hole, who spotted a visibly aroused elephant, complained that the sight of this rampant beast ruined his honeymoon by making him feel "inadequate".

Think she may have been the one disturbed.

A woman threatened to call police after claiming that she'd been locked in by staff. When in fact, she had mistaken the "do not disturb" sign on the back of the door as a warning to remain in the room

Really?

"The beach was too sandy."

White sand is so last year.

"We found the sand was not like the sand in the brochure. Your brochure shows the sand as yellow but it was white."

Did he use a ladle.

A guest at a Novotel in Australia complained his soup was too thick and strong. He was inadvertently slurping the gravy at the time.

He needs a pair of discreet sunglasses.

"Topless sunbathing on the beach should be banned. The holiday was ruined as my husband spent all day looking at other women."

I always thought they were real.

"We bought 'Ray-Ban' sunglasses for five Euro from a street trader, only to find out they were fake."

Or sand on the beach.

"No-one told us there would be fish in the sea. The children were startled."

That's why it is called a long haul holiday.

"It took us nine hours to fly home from Jamaica to England it only took the Americans three hours to get home."

You have to be kidding me?

"I compared the size of our one-bedroom apartment to our friends' three-bedroom apartment and ours was significantly smaller.."

No you won't, you failed the intelligence test.

"The brochure stated: 'No hairdressers at the accommodation'. We're trainee hairdressers - will we be OK staying there?"

Surely not?

"There are too many Spanish people. The receptionist speaks Spanish. The food is Spanish. Too many foreigners now live abroad."

Natures own.

"We had to queue outside with no air conditioning."

And of stupid guests, perhaps?

"It is your duty as a tour operator to advise us of noisy or unruly guests before we travel."

A way to eradicate Malaria.

"I was bitten by a mosquito, no-one said they could bite."

Oh my god, you've bred!

"My fiancé and I booked a twin-bedded room but we were placed in a double-bedded room. We now hold you responsible for the fact that I find myself pregnant. This would not have happened if you had put us in the room that we booked."

Flight attendants and crew have their own humour and occasionally like to display this to their customers. Below is a selection of the very best announcements from them.

Ah the Paul Simon classic.

"There may be 50 ways to leave your lover, but there are only 4 ways out of this airplane..."

But please leave the tray behind.

"Your seat cushions can be used for flotation, and in the event of an emergency water landing, please take them with our compliments."

Good luck with trying to light it.

"We do feature a smoking section on this flight; if you must smoke, please contact a member of the flight crew and they will escort you to the wing of the airplane."

Through the trap door.

"Smoking in the lavatories is prohibited. Any person caught smoking in the lavatories will be asked to leave the plane immediately."

No wing walking, please.

Pilot - "Folks, we have reached our cruising altitude now, so I am going to switch the seat belt sign off. Feel free to move about as you wish, but please stay inside the plane till we land… it's a bit cold outside, and if you walk on the wings it affects the flight pattern."

Sometimes honesty isn't the best policy.

And, after landing: "Thank you for flying Delta Business Express. We hope you enjoyed giving us the business as much as we enjoyed taking you for a ride."

Now, where are those latex gloves.

As we waited just off the runway for another airliner to cross in front of us, some of the passengers were beginning to retrieve luggage from the overhead bins. The head attendant announced on the intercom, This aircraft is equipped with a video surveillance system that monitors the cabin during taxiing. Any passengers not remaining in their seats until the aircraft comes to a full and complete stop at the gate will be strip-searched as they leave the aircraft.

One for the frightened flyers.

Once on a South west flight, the pilot said, "We've reached our cruising altitude now, and I'm turning off the seat belt sign. I'm switching to autopilot, too, so I can come back there and visit with all of you for the rest of the flight."

We hope they were talking about the plane!

As the plane landed and was coming to a stop at Washington National, a lone voice comes over the loudspeaker: "Whoa, big fella…WHOA..!"

And breathe.

"Should the cabin lose pressure, oxygen masks will drop from the overhead area. Please place the bag over your own mouth and nose before assisting children or adults acting like children."

Not forgetting the pilots too.

"As you exit the plane, please be sure to gather all of your belongings. Anything left behind will be distributed evenly among the flight attendants. Please do not leave children or spouses." "Last one off the plane must clean it."

Someone forgot his coffee.

And from the pilot during his welcome message: "We are pleased to have some of the best flight attendants in the industry…Unfortunately, none of them are on this flight…!

Blame game.

Heard on Southwest Airlines just after a very hard landing in Salt Lake City: The flight attendant came on the intercom and said, "That was quite a bump and I know what y'all are thinking. I'm here to tell you it wasn't the airline's fault, it wasn't the pilot's fault, it wasn't the flight attendants' fault…it was the asphalt!"

Best check for damage.

Overheard on an American Airlines flight into Amarillo, Texas, on a particularly windy and bumpy day. During the final approach the Captain was really having to fight it. After an extremely hard landing, the Flight Attendant came on the PA and announced, "Ladies and Gentlemen, welcome to Amarillo. Please remain in your seats with your seat belts fastened while the Captain taxis what's left of our airplane to the gate!"

G'day mate.

Another flight Attendant's comment on a less than perfect landing: "We ask you to please remain seated as Captain Kangaroo bounces us to the terminal."

All shook up.

After a particularly rough landing during thunderstorms in Memphis, a flight attendant on a Northwest flight announced: "Please take care when opening the overhead compartments because, after a landing like that. I'm sure that everything has shifted."

Choices, choices.

From a Southwest Airlines employee.... "Welcome aboard Southwest Flight XXX to YYY. To operate your seat belt, insert the metal tab into the buckle, and pull tight. It works just like every other seat belt, and if you don't know how to operate one, you probably shouldn't be out in public unsupervised. In the event of a sudden loss of cabin pressure, oxygen masks will drop from the ceiling. Stop screaming, grab the mask, and pull it over your face. If you have a small child travelling with you, secure your mask before assisting with theirs. If you are travelling with two small children, decide now which one you love more. Weather at our destination is 50 degrees with some broken clouds, but they'll try to have them fixed before we arrive. Thank you, and remember, nobody loves you, or your money, more than Southwest Airlines."

Dogfight at thirty five thousand feet.

An airline pilot wrote that on this particular flight he had hammered his ship into the runway really hard. The airline had a policy which required the first officer to stand at the door while the passengers exited, smile, and give them a "Thanks for flying XYZ airline." He said that in light of his bad landing, he had a hard time looking the passengers in the eye, thinking that someone would have a smart comment. Finally everyone had gotten off except for this little old lady, walking with a cane. She said, "Sonny, mind if I ask you a question?" "Why no Ma'am," said the pilot, "what is it?" The little old lady said, "Did we land or were we shot down?"

Captain Crash.

After a real crusher of a landing in Phoenix, the Flight Attendant came on with, "Ladies and Gentlemen, please remain in your seats until Captain Crash and the Crew have brought the aircraft to a screeching halt up against the gate. And, once the tire smoke has cleared and the warning bells are silent, we'll open the door and you can pick your way through the wreckage to the terminal.

Well when you put it like that.

Part of a Flight Attendant's arrival announcement: "We'd like to thank you folks for flying with us today. And, the next time you get the insane urge to go blasting through the skies in a pressurized metal tube, we hope you'll think of us here at US Airways."

Council Complaints

In the UK each area has its own local council which deals with issues relating to transport, health and hygiene and also housing. The following are extracts of complaints sent to councils and housing associations.

That is going to hurt!

I want some repairs done to my cooker as it has backfired and burnt my knob off.

Maybe a change of diet is needed.

I wish to report that tiles are missing from the outside toilet roof. I think it was bad wind the other night that blew them off.

As close as possible.

My lavatory seat is cracked, where do I stand.

What, the sink cannot write itself?

I am writing on behalf of my sink, which is coming away from the wall.

What you do in your own home is entirely your decision.

I request permission to remove my drawers in the kitchen.

Maths is obviously not this persons strong point.

50% of the walls are damp, 50% have crumbling plaster and the rest are plain filthy.

Hot pants.

I am still having problems with smoke in my new drawers.

Be careful not to flush them away.

The toilet is blocked and we cannot bath the children until it is cleared.

Maybe some form of protection?

Will you please send someone to mend the garden path. My wife tripped and fell on it yesterday and now she is pregnant. We are getting married in September and she would like it in the garden before we move house.

Any volunteers?

Will you please send a man to look at my water, it is a funny colour and not fit to drink.

Now if you have one thing and you split it two, oh forget it.

Our lavatory seat is broken in half and is now in three pieces.

Age concern.

Would you please send a man to repair my spout. I am an old age pensioner and need it badly.

A doodle doo.

I want to complain about the farmer across the road; every morning at 6a.m., his cock wakes me up and now it's getting too much for me.

Well he thinks it is impressive.

The man next door has a large erection in the back garden, which is unsightly and dangerous.

Right on it!

Our kitchen floor is damp. We have two children and would like a third, so please send someone round to do something about it.

A gag maybe?

I am a single woman living in a downstairs flat and would you please do something about the noise made by the man I have on top of me every night.

Not sure she would ever be satisfied.

Please send a man with the right tool to finish the job and satisfy my wife.

But he certainly has.

I have had the Clerk of the Works down on the floor six times, but I still have no satisfaction.

The lavatory seat / television aerial invention never really took off.

This is to let you know that our lavatory seat is broken and we can't get BBC2.

A hedge trimmer for the lady.

My bush is really overgrown around the front and my back passage has fungus growing in it.

Form a queue at the front please, ladies.

...and he's got this huge tool that vibrates the whole house and I just can't take any more.

Insurance

Next up on offer are some of the funniest motor insurance claims. These have been written by people filling in their claims forms after an accident.

Blues and twos

"I was driving along the motorway when the police pulled me over onto the hard shoulder. Unfortunately I was in the middle lane and there was another car in the way.."

Never!

"Going to work at 7am this morning I drove out of my drive straight into a bus. The bus was 5 minutes early.."

Skippy, is that you?

"I was driving along when I saw two kangaroos copulating in the middle of the road causing me to ejaculate through the sun roof."

Must have a strange pair of spectacles

"The accident happened because I had one eye on the lorry in front, one eye on the pedestrian and the other on the car behind.

That's called stopped.

"I started to slow down but the traffic was more stationary than I thought."

Fire dog.

"I pulled into a lay-by with smoke coming from under the hood. I realised the car was on fire so took my dog and smothered it with a blanket."

That would have worked.

Q: Could either driver have done anything to avoid the accident? A: Travelled by bus?

Yep, that's the sound a cow makes.

The claimant had collided with a cow. The questions and answers on the claim form were - Q: What warning was given by you? A: Horn. Q: What warning was given by the other party? A: Moo.

Natural wildlife of the UK.

"I started to turn and it was at this point I noticed a camel and an elephant tethered at the verge. This distraction caused me to lose concentration and hit a bollard."

Breaking bad.

"On approach to the traffic lights the car in front suddenly broke."

Not surprising really.

"I was going at about 70 or 80 mph when my girlfriend on the pillion reached over and grabbed my testicles so I lost control."

Or on a full moon.

"I didn't think the speed limit applied after midnight"

Puppy power!

"I knew the dog was possessive about the car but I would not have asked her to drive it if I had thought there was any risk."

Living on the edge.

Q: Do you engage in motorcycling, hunting or any other pastimes of a hazardous nature? A: "I Watch the Lottery Show and listen to Terry Wogan."

You can never take our freedom!

"First car stopped suddenly, second car hit first car and a haggis ran into the rear of second car."

Possibly.

"Windscreen broken. Cause unknown. Probably Voodoo."

Well you have to make sure.

"The car in front hit the pedestrian but he got up so I hit him again"

Fully understandable.

"I pulled away from the side of the road, glanced at my mother-in-law and headed over the embankment."

Maybe they should have text, oh wait..

"The other car collided with mine without giving warning of its intention."

The magically moving stationary vehicle.

"I collided with a stationary truck coming the other way"

Has she got a face like a rear end?

"A truck backed through my windshield into my wife's face"

Was he moving fast?

"A pedestrian hit me and went under my car"

That'll do it.

"In an attempt to kill a fly, I drove into a telephone pole."

Was it camouflaged?

"I had been shopping for plants all day and was on my way home. As I reached an intersection a hedge sprang up obscuring my vision and I did not see the other car."

That could be messy.

"I was on my way to the doctor with rear end trouble when my universal joint gave way causing me to have an accident."

Well it would. Wouldn't it.

"An invisible car came out of nowhere, struck my car and vanished."

Bovine search and rescue.

"I was thrown from the car as it left the road. I was later found in a ditch by some stray cows."

In a car you probably don't have now.

"Coming home I drove into the wrong house and collided with a tree I don't have."

Too clean.

"I thought my window was down, but I found it was up when I put my head through it."

Stay still damn it.

"The guy was all over the road. I had to swerve a number of times before I hit him."

A long drive.

"I had been driving for forty years when I fell asleep at the wheel and had an accident."

Maybe it had been knocked down before.

"As I approached an intersection a sign suddenly appeared in a place where no stop sign had ever appeared before."

The obvious choice.

"To avoid hitting the bumper of the car in front I struck a pedestrian."

Look up parked in the dictionary.

"My car was legally parked as it backed into another vehicle."

Hat'll be bad (I'll get my coat)

"I told the police that I was not injured, but on removing my hat found that I had a fractured skull."

Run Forrest, run.

"I was sure the old fellow would never make it to the other side of the road when I struck him."

But you still got him.

"The pedestrian had no idea which way to run as I ran over him."

No wonder he was sad.

"I saw a slow moving, sad faced old gentleman as he bounced off the roof of my car."

That paints a picture.

"The indirect cause of the accident was a little guy in a small car with a big mouth."

Pole to pole.

"The telephone pole was approaching. I was attempting to swerve out of the way when I struck the front end."

Fifty shades.

"The gentleman behind me struck me on the backside. He then went to rest in a bush with just his rear end showing.
"

U-turn

"I had been learning to drive with power steering. I turned the wheel to what I thought was enough and found myself in a different direction going the opposite way."

There was a warning there before I feel.

"I was backing my car out of the driveway in the usual manner, when it was struck by the other car in the same place it had been struck several times before."

Well if you going to crash, do it in style.

"When I saw I could not avoid a collision I stepped on the gas and crashed into the other car."

Magic door; Open!

"The accident happened when the right front door of a car came round the corner without giving a signal."

Thought you said no one was to blame.

"No one was to blame for the accident but it would never have happened if the other driver had been alert."

I wonder how many they sell?

"I was unable to stop in time and my car crashed into the other vehicle. The driver and passengers then left immediately for a vacation with injuries."

Too slow.

"The pedestrian ran for the pavement, but I got him."

Did you see the white of her eyes?

"I saw her look at me twice. She appeared to be making slow progress when we met on impact."

Well at least it stopped you skidding.

"The accident occurred when I was attempting to bring my car out of a skid by steering it into the other vehicle."

Crash deflectors.

"I bumped into a lamp-post which was obscured by human beings."

Deep sea diver.

"My car got hit by a submarine." (The Navy informed the wife of a submariner that the craft was due in port. She drove to the base to meet her husband and parked at the end of the slip where the sub was to berth. An inexperienced ensign was conning the sub and it rammed the end of the slip, breaking a section away, causing her car to fall into the water. The Navy paid the compensation claim.)

Courtroom.

And finally for this edition, we are going to leave you with some of the best courtroom quotes. These are all allegedly true but we will let you decide on their factual basis.

Sounds painful.

Q: "The truth of the matter is that you were not an unbiased, objective witness, isn't it? You too were shot in the fracas."
A: "No, sir. I was shot midway between the fracas and the naval."

Can't argue with that.

Q: What is your date of birth?
A: July fifteenth.
Q: What year?

A: Every year.

Snappy dresser.

Q: What gear were you in at the moment of the impact?
A: Gucci sweats and Reeboks.

I would but I can't remember.

Q: This myasthenia gravis, does it affect your memory at all?
A: Yes.
Q: And in what ways does it affect your memory?
A: I forget.
Q: You forget. Can you give us an example of something that you've forgotten?

Benjamin Button.

Q: How old is your son, the one living with you?
A: Thirty-eight or thirty-five, I can't remember which.
Q: How long has he lived with you?
A: Forty-five years.

Bad move.

Q: What was the first thing your husband said to you when he woke up that morning?
A: He said, "Where am I, Cathy?"
Q: And why did that upset you?
A: My name is Susan.

Yes, but do you?

Q: Do you know if your daughter has ever been involved in voodoo or the occult?
A: We both do.
Q: Voodoo?
A: We do.
Q: You do?
A: Yes, voodoo.

Unless you turn into a zombie.

Q: Now doctor, isn't it true that when a person dies in his sleep, he doesn't know about it until the next morning?

Er, 21 I guess.

Q: The youngest son, the twenty-year old, how old is he?

No I was out of town.

Q: Were you present when your picture was taken?

Take a guess.

Q: So the date of conception (of the baby) was August 8th?
A: Yes.
Q: And what were you doing at that time?

I'm just guessing, but I would say not.

Q: She had three children, right?
A: Yes.
Q: How many were boys?
A: None.

Q: Were there any girls?

Go figure.

Q: How was your first marriage terminated?
A: By death.
Q: And by whose death was it terminated?

Unless the circus is in town.

Q: Can you describe the individual?
A: He was about medium height and had a beard.
Q: Was this a male, or a female?

Is it just me or could I imagine Leslie Nielsen saying that.

Q: Doctor, how many autopsies have you performed on dead people?
A: All my autopsies are performed on dead people.

Well you said it.

Q: All your responses must be oral, OK? What school did you go to?
A: Oral.

That would be a shock.

Q: Do you recall the time that you examined the body?
A: The autopsy started around 8:30 p.m.
Q: And Mr Dennington was dead at the time?
A: No, he was sitting on the table wondering why I was doing an autopsy.

Are you qualified to practice law?

Q: Are you qualified to give a urine sample?

Way to go Doc.

Q: Doctor, before you performed the autopsy, did you check for a pulse?
A: No.
Q: Did you check for blood pressure?
A: No.
Q: Did you check for breathing?
A: No.
Q: So, then it is possible that the patient was alive when you began the autopsy?
A: No.
Q: How can you be so sure, Doctor?
A: Because his brain was sitting on my desk, in a jar.
Q: But could the patient have still been alive, never the less?
A: Yes, it is possible that he could have been alive and practising law somewhere.

Thank you reading this first edition of "Ridiculous customer complaints and other statements", we hope you enjoyed them and that they gave you a few laughs. We are busy working on the forthcoming editions, so if you have any stories you wish to share please feel free to contact us at the following :
ridiculouscomplaints@gmail.com

All stories are warmly and lovingly received, we do take care of them I can assure you! So help us and we will make sure you get a credit for them and you will see your name in print.

If you liked this book please feel free to leave a review, if you didn't like it then still feel free to leave a review and remember the author's name is J.K Rowling (Only kidding).

Printed in Great Britain
by Amazon